Living
with
Courage

Living with Courage

Lessons *from the* Life *of* Daniel

BILL CROWDER

Discovery House Publishers

Books, music, and videos that feed the soul with the Word of God

Box 3566 Grand Rapids, MI 49501

© 2006, 2008 by RBC Ministries
Grand Rapids, Michigan
All rights reserved.

Requests for permission to quote from this book should
be directed to: Permissions Department, Discovery House
Publishers, P.O. Box 3566, Grand Rapids, MI 49501.

Scripture quotations are from The New King James
Version, © 1982 by Thomas Nelson, Inc. All rights
reserved.

Interior design by Nick Richardson

ISBN: 978-1-57293-300-2

Printed in the United States of America
08 09 10 11 / 10 9 8 7 6 5 4 3 2 1

Contents

In Gratitude and Acknowledgment

When you write, you stand on the shoulders of those who have gone before you, modeling teaching in a way that impacts your own thinking. For me, such a person has been Dr. Donald K. Campbell, president emeritus of Dallas Theological Seminary. I fell in love with the idea of telling the stories of Bible characters as I absorbed his treatment of Daniel's life in his book *Daniel: Decoder of Dreams* and am indebted to him for his insights. I am grateful for his wisdom and practicality, for Campbell taught me the value of taking the words of the Scriptures and injecting them with the heart and life of the people whose experiences are described in those words. His example continues to influence my teaching ministry today, and I am grateful.

Introduction

In the 1960s, American citizens were fighting battles on a number of fronts. In Vietnam, American soldiers were dying in an unpopular war. At home, citizens were engaged in a series of conflicts, each of which wrote new chapters of American history. There were generational conflicts as young people began challenging every kind of authority, from universities and institutions to the hard-earned wealth that their parents' generation was bequeathing to them. There was racial conflict as an emerging African-American community bravely stood up to claim the equal rights granted to them by their country's constitution. There was violence that raged from campus protests to demonstrations at political conventions—and even the assassinations of social and government leaders. And there was religious conflict as the historic traditions of established, institutional churches were challenged by an enthusiastic youth-based movement calling itself the Jesus People.

This social upheaval foreshadowed social conflicts (Watergate, the Iran-Contra affair, abortion rights, the women's liberation movement, and more) that would seriously threaten the unity of the nation. The Culture Wars, as they came to be known, divided society over moral issues often linked to religious convictions. What begin as theoretically different views of God, the world, justice, humanness, and freedom, has resulted in radically divergent ways of living and dying. These faith-based differences radically affect the way people live their lives and the way society is shaped.

"In today's world, differences can be seen to make a difference. Beliefs have consequences."
–Os GUINNESS

In the past, some people of faith have withdrawn from society into insulated communities separated from the cultural fray (think of the Amish, the Quakers, some Mennonite groups, and others). Others have organized themselves into political action groups (think of the Moral Majority, Christian Coalition, or the American Coalition for Traditional Values). Still others have found themselves destined to show that, in the hand of God, one life can make a difference—even without the guarantee of civil rights, and even in the middle of a foreign culture (think of countless missionaries serving in tragically difficult cultures under the threat of death).

11

The Influence of One Life

About six hundred years before the birth of Christ, a man from Judah saw his nation overrun and his life uprooted. Together with a group of other Jewish captives, this man, Daniel, was taken from his homeland to a place called Babylon—a foreign culture hundreds of miles and light-years away from Jerusalem. In the region now known as Iraq, Daniel experienced the challenge of living out his faith in a culture devoted to a set of values and priorities that were vastly different from his own.

In this new world, Daniel and his friends lived out the convictions of their faith, which soon put them out of step with their powerful captors. Yet, in the middle of this pagan world, Daniel became a governmental leader, serving in appointed positions under three kings; a historian, recording what God did in his day; and a prophet who predicted the future and spoke truth to leaders.

For us, all these centuries later, Daniel is a case study of how one lives out personal faith in a hostile culture. In the following pages, we'll see that what God reveals about Himself in the unfolding drama of Daniel can put us in touch with the great timeless purposes of life.

Living a Life of Distinction

As Daniel's story opens, Judah is being invaded, just as the prophet Jeremiah foretold. For over twenty years Jeremiah had pled with the citizens of Judah to return to their God. If they refused, he warned, they would be captured by the Babylonians and taken captive for seventy years (Jeremiah 25:1–11). Because Judah had turned a deaf ear to these warnings, Daniel now writes as a witness to the invasion and describes what happened in its wake.

The King's Plan

In the third year of the reign of Jehoiakim king of Judah, Nebuchadnezzar king of

Babylon came to Jerusalem and besieged it.
And the Lord gave Jehoiakim king of Judah
into his hand, with some of the articles of the
house of God, which he carried into the land
of Shinar to the house of his god; and he
brought the articles into the treasure house
of his god (Daniel 1:1–2).

King Nebuchadnezzar of Babylon decided
to take the best and brightest of the captive
nation of Judah and use them to advance his
nation. Unlike Ahasuerus in the book of Esther,
who took women captive for his own personal
pleasure, Nebuchadnezzar chose the finest young
men to better his nation. He desired those with
the best minds and abilities to make Babylon
stronger. Because of this, the king's selection
process demanded that those selected meet high
standards.

Then the king instructed Ashpenaz, the master of his eunuchs, to bring some of the children of Israel and some of the king's descendants and some of the nobles, young men in whom there was no blemish, but good-looking, gifted in all wisdom, possessing knowledge and quick to understand, who had ability to serve in the king's palace, and whom they might teach the language and literature of the Chaldeans (1:3–4).

17

"People with courage and character always seem sinister to the rest."
—HERMAN HESSE

That's an impressive list! These young men had to be good-looking and without physical defect, they had to be both wise and able to learn, and they had to be capable of discernment.

The king was serious about this program.

These young men would be in training for three years before they were ready to serve him fully, and during that time they were treated well.

> And the king appointed for them a daily
> provision of the king's delicacies and of
> the wine which he drank, and three years
> of training for them, so that at the end
> of that time they might serve before the
> king. Now from among those of the sons
> of Judah were Daniel, Hananiah, Mishael,
> and Azariah. To them the chief of the
> eunuchs gave names: he gave Daniel the
> name Belteshazzar; to Hananiah, Shadrach;
> to Mishael, Meshach; and to Azariah, Abed-
> Nego (1:5-7).

Yes, Daniel, Hananiah, Mishael, and Azariah would be better off than the other captives who were now slaves in Babylon, but their situation produced its own challenges. These came in several forms:

Environment—In the midst of a pagan land and people, these young men, at an impressionable age, must maintain their purity.

Lifestyle—"The king's delicacies" were not necessarily a bad diet, but this was food and drink that had been offered and dedicated to Babylon's false gods. To eat that food and drink that wine was to endorse those idols.

Allegiance—The king's plan was a subtle attack on the very heart of their beliefs. By requiring that they study under the astrologers of Babylon, he hoped to change their thinking. By changing their names, he hoped to change their worship. Their Jewish names pointed to the God of Israel. The name changes were to indicate a shift in allegiance to the Babylonian gods.

By changing their way of thinking, eating, and worshiping, Nebuchadnezzar hoped to change their way of living. How would they respond to this character test?

Daniel's Response

But Daniel purposed in his heart that he would not defile himself with the portion of the king's delicacies, nor with the wine which he drank; therefore he requested of the chief of the eunuchs that he might not defile himself (1:8).

Daniel recognized that eating the king's food raised an issue of principle. He saw something about the food that prompted a response similar to what we find King David saying in Psalm 119: "Your word I have hidden in my heart, that I might not sin against You" (v. 11).

What did Daniel see? First of all, the king's food wasn't kosher: it was not prepared according to the dietary principles of Israel. Life in exile, however, made it impossible for the young men to keep many of the Torah- and temple-based laws of Israel. But what was probably a greater issue for Daniel was the fact that he didn't want to do anything that would honor the gods of Babylon (this pattern of principle would also show up in other areas of his life in captivity). Daniel considered eating and drinking food and wine offered to idols as a violation of the Word of God and the honor of his God.

21

The easy route would have been to go with the flow: "When in Babylon, do as the Babylonians do." But Daniel's objective was obedience, in spite of his environment.

"Fidelity to commitment in the face of doubts and fears is a very spiritual thing."

Notice that Daniel "purposed in his heart." This is the key attitude. If the priority is purity, you must have a *desire* to obey God and the *commitment* to act on that desire. Daniel had a variety of options, but he was determined to be true to his God.

A life committed to God begins with purpose of heart, and from the very beginning of the three-year training period, Daniel was tested on this issue.

> Now God had brought Daniel into the favor
> and goodwill of the chief of the eunuchs.
> And the chief of the eunuchs said to Daniel,
> "I fear my lord the king, who has appointed
> your food and drink. For why should he see
> your faces looking worse than the young men
> who are your age? Then you would endanger
> my head before the king" (1:9–10).

In defense of the chief eunuch, his was not a terribly tolerant responsibility. Had he varied from the king's instructions, and it backfired, he could lose his own life. He was undoubtedly in a difficult situation. But God had made preparation for this moment. He had given Daniel favor with the chief of the eunuchs. We don't know exactly how—perhaps it was Daniel's demeanor with his captors—but God had been at work behind the scenes. And Daniel reinforced this favor by using diplomacy, even as he took his stand.

Daniel said to the steward who had been put in charge of him:

23

> "Please test your servants for ten days, and let them give us vegetables to eat and water to drink. Then let our appearance be examined before you, and the appearance of the young men who eat the portion of the king's delicacies; and as you see fit, so deal with your servants." So he consented with them in this matter, and tested them ten days (1:12–14).

Daniel went to the warden and asked for a ten-day trial diet of vegetables. I'm a meat-and-potatoes kind of guy, so this isn't very attractive to me. Ten days of vegetables? Not for me. Beyond that, however, this test required a kind of suspension of the laws of nutrition. How could there be a noticeable difference in only ten days? It was a small test of faith that would prepare Daniel for the greater tests of faith to come.

> *"In prosperity our friends know us; in adversity we know our friends."*
> —JOHN CHURTON COLLINS

God's Deliverance

The test worked and showed that Daniel and his friends knew what Israel forgot—God blesses obedience.

At the end of ten days their features appeared
better and fatter in flesh than all the young
men who ate the portion of the king's
delicacies. Thus the steward took away their
portion of delicacies and the wine that they
were to drink, and gave them vegetables
(1:15-16).

Daniel and his friends came out better than
the others who were in the king's training
program because God worked on their behalf.
As a result, the vegetable diet was allowed to
continue (though, to me, that would be more of a
punishment than a reward!).

Because Daniel was committed to a purity that
flowed from obedience to God's Word, he had a
strong foundation for living in a difficult culture.

As for these four young men, God gave them
knowledge and skill in all literature and

wisdom; and Daniel had understanding in
all visions and dreams. Now at the end of the
days, when the king had said that they should
be brought in, the chief of the eunuchs
brought them in before Nebuchadnezzar.
Then the king interviewed them, and
among them all none was found like Daniel,
Hananiah, Mishael, and Azariah; therefore
they served before the king

26

And in all matters of wisdom and
understanding, about which the king
examined them, he found them ten times
better than all the magicians and astrologers
who were in all his realm (1:17–20).

At the end of their training, God's blessing is
confirmed as Daniel and his friends are declared
to be "ten times better" than all the scholars of
Babylon.

Daniel was probably no more than twenty

years old at this point, which means he was only sixteen or seventeen when he was initially put to the test. At that young age, he was set apart for service and lived a life of distinction in a powerful pagan culture of the ancient world.

Living a Life of Confidence

What do the following people and situations have in common?

- A goalkeeper for a World Cup soccer team in a penalty kick shootout
- A surgeon in the midst of a difficult heart-bypass procedure
- An airline pilot trying to land a jet with two of the engines out

All of these challenging situations demand that the individuals involved perform at the highest level of skill in moments of great pressure and scrutiny. And this is where we find Daniel and his friends as the story continues. They will rise above the pressure with a deep confidence in God.

The Stage Is Set

Now in the second year of Nebuchadnezzar's reign, Nebuchadnezzar had dreams; and his spirit was so troubled that his sleep left him (Daniel 2:1).

This verse perfectly illustrates Shakespeare's line in *Henry IV*: "Uneasy lies the head that wears a crown." Nebuchadnezzar's sleep was disturbed by dreams. But it was one particular dream that concerned him. As theologian Donald Campbell put it, the cares of the day became the cares of the night, and the king awoke in turmoil and summoned his advisors.

The king called "the magicians, the

"No pressure, no diamonds."
—MARY CASE

astrologers, the sorcerers, and the Chaldeans" (2:2). The magicians were the sacred writers or scholars. The astrologers were enchanters and sacred priests. The sorcerers were involved in the occult and sold herbs and potions. And the Chaldeans were the king's wise men. (The king did not call Daniel and friends, so they were probably still in training at the time.)

Once they were all assembled before the king, a dialogue ensued that showed these alleged wise men just how much trouble they were in.

And the king said to them, "I have had a dream, and my spirit is anxious to know the dream."

Then the Chaldeans spoke to the king in Aramaic, "O king, live forever! Tell your

31

servants the dream, and we will give the interpretation."

The king answered and said to the Chaldeans, "My decision is firm: if you do not make known the dream to me, and its interpretation, you shall be cut in pieces, and your houses shall be made an ash heap. However, if you tell the dream and its interpretation, you shall receive from me gifts, rewards, and great honor. Therefore tell me the dream and its interpretation."

They answered again and said, "Let the king tell his servants the dream, and we will give its interpretation."

The king answered and said, "I know for certain that you would gain time, because you see that my decision is firm: if you do not make known the dream to me, there is only one decree for you! For you have agreed to speak lying and corrupt words before me till

the time has changed. Therefore tell me the
dream, and I shall know that you can give me
its interpretation" (2:3-9).

That is dramatic. I am convinced that the
king had been suspicious of these rascals for
some time. He no doubt had wondered at the
"yes-men" attitudes they brought in the place of
wise counsel. As a result, he held his ground in
the face of their protests and threatened them
with death if they failed to come through with
his demand for an accurate interpretation of the
dream.

Their plea for mercy revealed the seriousness
of the danger they were in:

The Chaldeans answered the king, and said,
"There is not a man on earth who can tell
the king's matter; therefore no king, lord,
or ruler has ever asked such things of any

33

magician, astrologer, or Chaldean. It is a
difficult thing that the king requests, and
there is no other who can tell it to the king
except the gods, whose dwelling is not with
flesh."

For this reason the king was angry and
very furious, and gave the command to
destroy all the wise men of Babylon. So the
decree went out, and they began killing the
wise men; and they sought Daniel and his
companions, to kill them (2:10-13).

After the wise men admitted their inability to
interpret Nebuchadnezzar's dream, he exploded.
He was so enraged that he ordered all the wise
men—including Daniel and the other young men
in training—to be executed. As a result, Daniel
and his friends were arrested.

But when the Chaldeans told the king that his
request was unfair because only the gods could

do such a thing, they unwittingly set the stage for
Daniel's God to do just that!

The Submissive Hearts

Arioch, the captain of the king's guard, was
sent out to kill all the wise men of Babylon. But
when he approached Daniel, the young Hebrew
was able to speak to him "with counsel and
wisdom" (2:14). Daniel asked for an explanation,
and Arioch told him the entire sad story. Making
the most of the opportunity,

35

> Daniel went in and asked the king to give
> him time, that he might tell the king the
> interpretation (2:16).

Essentially, Daniel said, "Give me time, and I
guarantee the king an answer." This was a huge
promise!

Then Daniel went to
his house, and made
the decision known to
Hananiah, Mishael,

*"Lord, I believe;
help my unbelief!"*
—MARK 9:24

and Azariah, his companions, that they
might seek mercies from the God of heaven
concerning this secret, so that Daniel and his
companions might not perish with the rest of
the wise men of Babylon (2:17–18).

36

Daniel shared his burden with his friends, and
together they began praying. They began to "seek
mercies from the God of heaven." This was a
powerful expression of their spiritual confidence.
They desired that God in His mercy would
intervene and rescue them from the execution
that had been planned.

Then the secret was revealed to Daniel in a
night vision. So Daniel blessed the God of

heaven. Daniel answered and said: "Blessed be the name of God forever and ever, for wisdom and might are His. And He changes the times and the seasons; He removes kings and raises up kings; He gives wisdom to the wise and knowledge to those who have understanding. He reveals deep and secret things; He knows what is in the darkness, and light dwells with Him. I thank You and praise You, O God of my fathers; You have given me wisdom and might, and have now made known to me what we asked of You, for You have made known to us the king's demand" (2:19–23).

As the young men prayed, God unveiled the secret of the king's dream to Daniel. Notice the matter-of-fact statement of this answer to prayer: "Then the secret was revealed." Notice also Daniel's response. With the proverbial noose

still around his neck, his first response was not
to gain relief or to use his knowledge to his own
advantage. Rather, it was to worship. And the
focus of that worship was the God of power and
provision:

- "Blessed be the name of God," which is an
  emblem of God's character;
- "Wisdom and might are His," not Daniel's;
- "He changes the times and the seasons,"
  implying total control over all of life;
- "He removes kings and raises up kings," for
  God is sovereign over the nations;
- "He gives wisdom . . . and knowledge," as is
  promised in James 1:5;
- "He reveals deep and secret things,"
  including this dream;
- "He knows what is in the darkness, and
  light dwells with Him."

> *"What comes into our minds when we think about God is the most important thing about us."*
> —A. W. TOZER

Daniel gave God all the praise for answering his prayer. What a marvelous display of worship!

Would it have been inappropriate for Daniel to thank God for saving his life? Of course not. But it seems that even this miraculous rescue was secondary in Daniel's mind to the wonder of the God who performed it.

39

Daniel's response should cause each of us to examine our heart to see where our own focus would have been:

- on the blessings or on the Blesser?
- on the work or on the Lord of the work?
- on the answer to prayer or on the God who answers prayer?

It's all about focus. And when we fail to put our confidence in God, it's easy to lose our focus. Our perspective becomes blurred, and we see the trees rather than the forest. Yet Daniel's focus stayed clear during a time of life-and-death pressure. His heart was locked in on his God, and God enabled him to perform rather than wilt under pressure.

The Secret Revealed

Daniel moved ahead in confidence that God would prepare the way.

> Therefore Daniel went to Arioch, whom the king had appointed to destroy the wise men of Babylon. He went and said thus to him: "Do not destroy the wise men of Babylon; take me before the king, and I will tell the king the interpretation." Then Arioch quickly brought Daniel before the king, and

said thus to him, "I have found a man of the captives of Judah, who will make known to the king the interpretation" (2:24-25).

Daniel went to Arioch, the captain of the king's guard, and told him that he could interpret the king's dream and that he should not kill the wise men. Arioch, at Daniel's request, took him to the king, and when Daniel stood before the royal presence (apparently for the first time), the king asked a pointed and compelling question:

> "Are you able to make known to me the dream which I have seen, and its interpretation?" (2:26).

In other words, was Daniel able to succeed where all of the king's wise men had failed? The answer was a definitive yes.

"The secret which the king has demanded,
the wise men, the astrologers, the magicians,
and the soothsayers cannot declare to the
king. But there is a God in heaven who
reveals secrets, and He has made known to
King Nebuchadnezzar what will be in the
latter days. . . . He who reveals secrets has
made known to you what will be. But as for
me, this secret has not been revealed to me
because I have more wisdom than anyone
living, but for our sakes who make known
the interpretation to the king, and that
you may know the thoughts of your heart"
(2:27–30).

This was not false humility on Daniel's part.
It was a sincere understanding of his role in the
event. The issue was clear—it was about God, not
Daniel. And his actions revealed the trust he had
in God.

*   *   *

Daniel was able to accurately interpret Nebuchadnezzar's dream, which was a powerful learning opportunity for the king. But even more powerful was the glory this brought to Daniel's God:

> The king answered Daniel, and said, "Truly your God is the God of gods, the Lord of kings, and a revealer of secrets, since you could reveal this secret" (2:47).

In life, as with weather, there are times of high pressure or low pressure—but there are never times of no pressure. Our choices during these changing times tell a lot about us.

Where is your focus in times of pressure? Are you scrambling to protect yourself at all costs? Are you doing desperate things that harm others in the process? Or are you more concerned about how your actions will reflect on your God?

In your thoughtful moments, ask God to showcase His presence in your life. Use these moments to line up with the eternal purposes and honor of God.

Living a Life of
Concern

There are two types of concern. The first type stands at a distance from situations of pain or tragedy, shaking its head in dismay and saying things like, "How sad. What a shame. Why doesn't someone do something about this?" The second type of concern is the someone who seeks to do something about it.

Concern can be a great motivator, as it was for Clara Barton. Disturbed by the lack of medicines and proper treatment for soldiers wounded in the American Civil War, Barton began providing medical aid and ambulances to the battlefronts. Her efforts and involvement, the physical expressions of her concern, saved countless lives and displayed a wonderful humanity in the midst of one of the most inhuman events in American history. Ultimately, her work became the foundation for the American Red Cross which, over 150 years later, continues to "do something about it" when there is need in communities and lives. It is about an active concern that is willing to get involved.

For some thirty years, Daniel has been a captive in Babylon. Having arrived in the city of his exile as a teenager, Daniel is now in his mid-forties. During his time in Babylon, he has stayed true to his God, but has also become a friend to his captor, Nebuchadnezzar. We can be certain, I think, that Daniel has prayed for this man and modeled a relationship with God before him. As a result, Nebuchadnezzar has been challenged and confronted. But, though he has been stirred, the great king remains unchanged. Unchanged, that is, until Nebuchadnezzar's world is rocked and Daniel gets involved. His heart of concern for his friend will not allow him to sit on the sidelines and watch.

The Conclusion at the Beginning

As we read this part of Daniel's story, we find that he plays two roles: he is the stenographer, recording the testimony of Nebuchadnezzar, and he is also part of the story he is recording. It begins:

47

Nebuchadnezzar the king,

To all peoples, nations, and languages that dwell in all the earth:

Peace be multiplied to you.

I thought it good to declare the signs and wonders that the Most High God has worked for me. How great are His signs, and how mighty His wonders! His kingdom is an

everlasting kingdom, and His dominion is
from generation to generation (Daniel 4:1–3).

For a pagan king, this is a rather startling
declaration. It signals a shift in his allegiance
away from the pantheon of the idol gods of
Babylon and to the God of Abraham, Isaac, and
Jacob. What contributed to this shift? Certainly
the things he has seen through Daniel and his
friends as he cites "signs" (perhaps the dreams
and visions described in chapters 1 and 2) and
"wonders" (perhaps the fiery furnace of Daniel
3) have played a role. But all of these things
culminate in the events of Daniel 4.

As he begins to tell his story, Nebuchadnezzar,
the proud king who has sought to build an
eternal kingdom in his own name, acknowledges
that God's "kingdom is an everlasting kingdom"
(4:3). This once arrogant, self-sufficient man now,
in honest humility, sees and declares his own

"It is doubtful whether God can bless a man greatly until He's hurt him deeply."
—A. W. TOZER

weakness. Nebuchadnezzar tells of his own crushing, as he shares events that will also break the heart of his friend, Daniel, with concern.

A Dangerous Situation

When I was a kid, one of the popular television shows was *Lost in Space*, in which the Robinsons—a family of space travelers—was thrown off course in outer space. As the Robinsons tried to survive countless dangers and adventures, they sometimes experienced threats because of the escapades of their precocious son, Will. To make it even worse, more often than not Will got in trouble because he ignored the warnings of their robot-companion who would trumpet, "Warning! Warning! Danger, Will Robinson, danger!" In spite of those clarion

49

calls, Will inevitably got in trouble anyway, and another adventure would hold us spellbound in front of our TVs.

Unfortunately, danger doesn't always come with warning labels. It usually sneaks up on us quietly, and then assaults us when we are least prepared for it. Such is the case with Nebuchadnezzar:

> I, Nebuchadnezzar, was at rest in my house,
> and flourishing in my palace. I saw a dream
> which made me afraid, and the thoughts
> on my bed and the visions of my head
> troubled me. Therefore I issued a decree to
> bring in all the wise men of Babylon before
> me, that they might make known to me
> the interpretation of the dream. Then the
> magicians, the astrologers, the Chaldeans,
> and the soothsayers came in, and I told them
> the dream; but they did not make known to
> me its interpretation (4:4–7).

The king is caught off guard completely. Like David when he succumbed to Bathsheba's charms, Nebuchadnezzar is "at rest." This means he is not at war; there are no enemies on the horizon to keep him sharp and alert. He is "flourishing in [his] palace,"—resting on his laurels, kicked back, enjoying success! He has spent countless lives and numerous fortunes building an empire for his own glory. Talk about worshiping the "god of self"—Nebuchadnezzar could be the poster child for that life view! In fact, he is so self-consumed that in two sentences alone (vv. 4–5) he uses first-person pronouns (I, me, my, mine) no fewer than eight times!

He is secure in his conquests and secure in his position—but completely insecure in his heart. There is a reckoning coming—and, once again, it comes in a dream.

> *"Delusions of grandeur make me feel a lot better about myself."*
> —JANE WAGNER

His sleep is interrupted by a dream that, as he himself describes, leaves him "afraid" and "troubled." These are the signs of a distressed heart that desperately needs relief.

What does he do? He looks for answers—but not from his friend Daniel. Instead, as he did years earlier, the king calls for the Chaldean wise men. Perhaps he was afraid of what Daniel would tell him, or perhaps he thought he could still control the Chaldeans. The reality, however, is that Nebuchadnezzar fails to consult the one man who can give him truthful answers—and perhaps the one man who genuinely cares about him.

Once again the Chaldeans fail to be able to interpret the dream, and once again Daniel comes center stage.

A Disturbing Dream

On August 28, 1963, Martin Luther King, Jr. delivered his famous I Have a Dream speech from the steps of the Lincoln Memorial in Washington DC. In it, King shared his dream of a nation of racial equality and justice, a land of wholeness and peace. It was a dream that gave hope to many, and focus to the civil rights movement.

Nebuchadnezzar's dream could not have been more different. It was one of anguish and suffering, rather than hope and peace. No wonder it disturbed him so greatly.

In his dream, the king saw a tree in the midst of the earth, very tall. Its foliage was beautiful and its fruit abundant, and all living creatures found shelter, protection, and sustenance in its branches and under its leaves (4:10–12). Sounds peaceful, doesn't it?

But then "a watcher" descended from heaven and issued commands that were ominous at best:

- Chop down the tree and cut off its branches (v. 14)

- Strip off its leaves and scatter its fruit (v. 14)
- Drive the birds from its branches, and the animals from under it (v. 14)
- Leave the stump and bind it with bronze (v. 15)

Notice that toward the end of verse 15 the pronoun changes from "it" to "he." The tree is not actually a tree; it represents *someone*, not something.

Nebuchadnezzar has no idea what this means, but he is deeply disturbed by what he has seen. He concludes the description of the dream by acknowledging that he has no doubts about Daniel's ability to interpret this dream—for better or for worse.

A Deep Concern

Daniel, too, is greatly disturbed by this dream—so affected that he is unable to even speak for a while.

> Then Daniel, whose name was Belteshazzar, was astonished for a time, and his thoughts troubled him (4:19a).

Daniel sees what is coming, and he is devastated by it. He aches inside over the things that he must say to his friend.

Sometimes hard truths or difficult things must be said—and often they are just as painful to speak as they are to hear. Daniel cannot be dispassionate. His deep affection for the king draws forth deep concern for the welfare of his friend.

55

> "When someone allows you to bear his burdens, you have found deep friendship."
> —REAL LIVE PREACHER

Notice that Nebuchadnezzar also shows concern for Daniel. He sees his distress and tries to let him off the hook. It is fascinating to me how these men have grown close over the years in spite of their obvious differences.

> The king spoke and said, "Belteshazzar, do not let the dream or its interpretation trouble you" (4:19b).

Daniel is grieved. He knows the dream favors the king's enemies. Yet he knows he must share the interpretation of the dream.

The tree is the king (4:20–22). It is Nebuchadnezzar's own future that is being foretold in this terrifying dream. The watcher is an angel, seen here as an instrument of divine judgment (4:23). And the message of the dream is harsh (4:24–27). Daniel says to the king:

- You will endure seven years of utter humiliation.
- They will drive you from men.

- You will dwell with the beasts, and eat as they do.
- Seven periods of time will pass until you learn the needed lesson. (Scholars believe this refers to seven years that will pass *until* the king learns the needed lesson, *until* he deals with the problem issues, *until* he confesses his pride. "Until" is a huge word. It is a word of hope and purpose, but not necessarily a word of brevity.)

These are harsh words, but the purpose is to teach the arrogant and proud king Nebuchadnezzar to humble himself before almighty God—and the stump is left to show that the king will return, but never to his former glory.

Daniel's response expresses his concern. He can't just stand by and watch. He can't just let his friend destroy himself. He must get involved. Daniel pleads with Nebuchadnezzar to repent.

> Therefore, O king, let my advice be
> acceptable to you; break off your sins by being
> righteous, and your iniquities by showing
> mercy to the poor. Perhaps there may be a
> lengthening of your prosperity (4:27).

58

God is a God who loves to show mercy ("for I know that You are a gracious and merciful God, slow to anger and abundant in lovingkindness, One who relents from doing harm" Jonah 4:2). Daniel begs the king to turn from his sin and to God in repentance—but Nebuchadnezzar does not repent.

A Great Downfall

All this came upon King Nebuchadnezzar (4:28).

Though Nebuchadnezzar is telling his own story, there is a candor and simplicity in this statement. Also, God, in mercy, allows the king a year of grace ("at the end of the twelve months," 4:29)—a window for repentance—but the king refuses to repent. Not only that, Nebuchadnezzar continues to seek his own glory—and it is that pride that becomes his downfall. He declares with self-satisfaction:

> "Is not this great Babylon, that I have built
> for a royal dwelling by my mighty power and
> for the honor of my majesty?" (4:30).

But the king's declaration of pride is followed by God's declaration of judgment (4:31–32), and the warning of the dream comes true: the king spends the next seven years living as if he were a wild beast (4:33). He eats grass like cattle, because that is what he has become! Medically this is an actual condition, referred to as zoanthropy, boanthropy, or lycanthropy. R. K. Harrison described the behavior of a man in a British mental institution who had this condition:

> His daily routine consisted of wandering around the magnificent lawns with which the otherwise dingy grounds were graced, and it was his custom to pluck up and eat handfuls of grass as he went along . . . he never ate institutionalized food with the other inmates, and his only drink was water . . . the only physical abnormality noted consisted of a lengthening of the hair and a coarse, thickening condition of the fingernails. Without institutional care the patient would have manifested precisely the same physical conditions as those mentioned in Daniel 4:33. (Cited in Donald K. Campbell, *Daniel: Decoder of Dreams*, p. 52.)

Imagine seven years of this degrading, humiliating life—and not even realizing it is happening to you! Imagine also, day in and day out, Nebuchadnezzar's political enemies gloating over his demise. And imagine, as well, Daniel standing on the balcony of the palace with Nebuchadnezzar's wife, the grieving queen Amytis, as they watch the king living like an animal—a beast.

For seven years, Nebuchadnezzar is humbled. For seven years, Daniel grieves.

A Great Mercy

Now, flash forward seven years, remembering that this is not third-person observation. This is Nebuchadnezzar's own testimony! After seven years of public humiliation, the "until" finally arrives:

And at the end of the time I,
Nebuchadnezzar, lifted my eyes to heaven,

and my understanding returned to me;
and I blessed the Most High and praised
and honored Him who lives forever: For
His dominion is an everlasting dominion,
and His kingdom is from generation to
generation (4:34).

The arrogance is gone, replaced with a clear
understanding of the person and greatness of
God. What a change! Now, instead of asserting
his own power, Nebuchadnezzar affirms that no
one can claim the honor due to God, and God
alone.

King Nebuchadnezzar
would never be the same,
for he had at last met
the God he had heard so
much about from the lips
of his friend, Daniel.

*"Life is a long
lesson in
humility."*
—JAMES M. BARRIE

*   *   *

In the midst of suffering what is needed most is not a clear view of the suffering, but a clear view of the God who is above the suffering. This is the God that Nebuchadnezzar now knows. A powerful, eternal lesson—learned in the most painful of ways.

In another time of suffering, another king (David) lamented his experience of solitary suffering with these words:

> Look on my right hand and see,
>> For there is no one who acknowledges me;
>> Refuge has failed me;
>> No one cares for my soul (Psalm 142:4).

But Nebuchadnezzar did not have to walk his path of pain alone. In Daniel, he had a concerned, caring friend to walk with him. As he had been for some thirty years, Daniel was at his side—challenging, helping, supporting, and counseling. Even more, not only had Daniel been a friend and confidant, he had been a difference-maker. Daniel's consistent, faithful example had brought an eternal spiritual impact in the life of the king. Daniel was willing to get involved and be an influence for God in his generation—even under extraordinarily difficult circumstances. He was willing to be engaged.

Edmund Burke said, "All that is necessary for the triumph of evil is that good men do nothing." This is a powerful reminder that we cannot afford to display the kind of remote concern that stands on the sidelines and laments, but remains at a distance. It is a reminder that, like Daniel, we must display the concern that steps in, holds on, and seeks to help.

Living a Life of Courage

Coming of age in the 1960s was "a bracing privilege," writes Os Guinness in *The Call*. No one could take anything for granted. For thinking people, everything was challenged and taken back to square one. "Nowhere was this challenge more plain than in knowing what we believed and why."

This was my generation—and everything held dear by the "establishment" and the older generation was not merely seen as optional, it was viewed as an oppressive structure that needed dismantling. The values and priorities of my parents' world were challenged and largely rejected by a generation that had not lived through the life-forming experiences of the Great Depression and World War II. There was little interest in understanding how the status quo had been achieved; there was simply a desire to challenge it, resist it, and remove its authority.

Similarly, in Daniel's lifetime he had seen many things. As a youth he had been taken from hearth and home in Jerusalem to pagan Babylon. He had been set aside for royal service and had risen to the role of a key advisor to the king, Nebuchadnezzar, seeing the evidence of God's involvement every step of the way. Of all the fascinating experiences that Daniel lived through, however, one of the most significant was the life-transforming spiritual awakening of the king. We can only imagine how the change in the king may have changed his kingdom, but in the ensuing years Nebuchadnezzar's rule would have certainly been modified by his awareness of the sovereignty of the King of heaven. I find myself imagining a golden age in Babylon with a king no longer ruthless but just. Not merely powerful, but honorable. A new paradigm.

Any such establishment of justice and honor, however, would have died with Nebuchadnezzar. His ultimate replacement was a man whose heart was the antithesis of all that Nebuchadnezzar had come to believe. Like the generation of our 1960s, instead of cherishing his heritage, he challenged it.

A New King

As we look at Daniel's ongoing experiences in Babylon, we see a new king—a man who challenged everything, especially the God whom Nebuchadnezzar had turned to years before (Daniel 4:34-37). And, he sought to do all he could to embrace the opposites, reverting the kingdom to the paganism Nebuchadnezzar had abandoned in order to submit to Daniel's God.

The year was 538 BC, twenty-three years after Nebuchadnezzar's death. The new king was Nebuchadnezzar's grandson Belshazzar, a man devoted to any god but the true God. It was a devotion that would bring both his downfall and the destruction of his kingdom.

The city of Babylon was under siege by the armies of the Medo-Persian empire. But the king was behaving strangely. Like Nero, the Roman emperor who fiddled while Rome burned, Belshazzar ordered a national holiday—in spite of the siege that threatened the city.

> Belshazzar the king made a great feast for a thousand of his lords, and drank wine in the presence of the thousand (Daniel 5:1).

Why such carefree revelry at a time like this? Several reasons are possible. First, the king wanted to put the people at ease, to reassure them that he was in control of the situation. Like someone who nervously whistles his way through a graveyard, the king attempted to create an atmosphere of confidence in spite of the danger. Second, Belshazzar wanted to show the authority of his kingdom. Third, he wanted to celebrate the Babylonian gods. These gods were displayed on the walls of the banquet hall, and Belshazzar led in toasting each of them in turn.

"You cannot escape the responsibility of tomorrow by evading it today."
—ABRAHAM LINCOLN

69

Then, when everyone was drunk, the king made his fatal mistake.

While he tasted the wine, Belshazzar gave the command to bring the gold and silver vessels which his father Nebuchadnezzar had taken from the temple which had been in Jerusalem, that the king and his lords, his wives, and his concubines might drink from them. Then they brought the gold vessels that had been taken from the temple of the house of God which had been in Jerusalem; and the king and his lords, his wives, and his concubines drank from them. They drank wine, and praised the gods of gold and silver, bronze and iron, wood and stone (5:2–4).

70

Remember, the kingdom is under siege and the king is trying to somehow prop up his shaky realm. So, in a drunken stupor, he calls for the temple vessels that were taken from Jerusalem years before. Why would he do this? Perhaps he wished to defy the God of Israel. Perhaps he wanted to prove that the old prophecy (from Daniel to Belshazzar's grandfather) of Babylon's demise was false. Perhaps he remembered how

> *"It is easier to exclude harmful passions than to rule them, and to deny them admittance than to control them after they have been admitted."*
> —SENECA

Daniel had humbled Nebuchadnezzar and wanted to show his own superiority.

Whatever the reason, in a time when Belshazzar should have been fasting instead of feasting, he showed his utter contempt for the Most High God. He toasted his idols with vessels intended for the worship of God.

A New Challenge

Belshazzar's blasphemy did not go unnoticed, and the consequences were immediate. They say that "what goes around, comes around." For Belshazzar, it was coming around!

In the same hour the fingers of a man's hand

appeared and wrote opposite the lampstand
on the plaster of the wall of the king's palace;
and the king saw the part of the hand that
wrote. Then the king's countenance changed,
and his thoughts troubled him, so that the
joints of his hips were loosened and his
knees knocked against each other. The king
cried aloud to bring in the astrologers, the
Chaldeans, and the soothsayers. The king
spoke, saying to the wise men of Babylon,
"Whoever reads this writing, and tells me
its interpretation, shall be clothed with
purple and have a chain of gold around his
neck; and he shall be the third ruler in the
kingdom" (5:5-7).

Belshazzar suddenly sobered up. He became
pale and weak, and his knees knocked together.
Earlier, he had been too drunk to stand. Now he
was too frightened to!

He immediately offered a reward to anyone who could interpret the writing, and what a reward it was! Belshazzar had received stewardship of the throne because, history tells us, his father, King Nabonidus, had gone mad and had been removed to the summer palace at Shushan. With his father still living, and Belshazzar manning the throne in his absence, "the third ruler" was the highest place of power in the kingdom!

Despite this more than magnanimous offer, all his wise men failed, and the king "was greatly troubled, his countenance was changed, and his lords were astonished" (5:8-9). Now Belshazzar faced a situation that he couldn't control, and he lost control.

Then, a solution came from an unlikely place.

The queen, because of the words of the king and his lords, came to the banquet hall. The

queen spoke, saying, "O king, live forever!
Do not let your thoughts trouble you, nor let
your countenance change. There is a man in
your kingdom in whom is the Spirit of the
Holy God. And in the days of your father,
light and understanding and wisdom, like
the wisdom of the gods, were found in him;
and King Nebuchadnezzar your father—your
father the king—made him chief of the
magicians, astrologers, Chaldeans, and
soothsayers. Inasmuch as an excellent spirit,
knowledge, understanding, interpreting
dreams, solving riddles, and explaining
enigmas were found in this Daniel, whom
the king named Belteshazzar, now let Daniel
be called, and he will give the interpretation"
(5:10–12).

The queen knew history. But notice who
she was. She was not the queen, the wife of

Belshazzar, for we are told that the king's wives
were already in the banqueting hall (5:3), even
though that was seen as shameful and a violation
of royal etiquette. Nor was she the queen, the
wife of King Nabonidus, for that queen was at
Shushan caring for her troubled husband. No,
this was undoubtedly the queen mother, Amytis,
the wife of Nebuchadnezzar. He had loved her so
passionately that he had constructed the hanging
gardens of Babylon, one of the seven wonders
of the ancient world, so that she would not be
homesick for her home in the lush green hill
country. She had lived through the experiences
of King Nebuchadnezzar (Daniel 4) and fully
understood what had happened, and how. She
not only knew her history—she had lived it!

A New Opportunity

Daniel, now an old man in his early eighties,
was brought to the king. What a scene! Imagine

Daniel standing there in the midst of this
banquet hall with its idolatry and immorality,
before this king who is defying the God he loves
and worships. Imagine what was in the heart of
this godly man who had sought to live a life of
purity.

Belshazzar offered Daniel both flattery and
great reward for interpreting the handwriting on
the wall.

> I have heard of you, that the Spirit of God
> is in you, and that light and understanding
> and excellent wisdom are found in you.
> Now the wise men, the astrologers, have
> been brought in before me, that they should
> read this writing and make known to me its
> interpretation, but they could not give the
> interpretation of the thing. And I have heard
> of you, that you can give interpretations
> and explain enigmas. Now if you can read

the writing and make known to me its interpretation, you shall be clothed with purple and have a chain of gold around your neck, and shall be the third ruler in the kingdom (5:14-16).

Notice that Daniel did not display the same level of compassion for this king that he had once shown to Nebuchadnezzar. He flatly refused the king's gifts and exposed his sin. With Nebuchadnezzar, he had counseled with compassion. With Belshazzar, he preached with honest fury.

> *"Where is there dignity unless there is honesty?"*
> —CICERO

Daniel told the king to keep his gifts. Then he proceeded to give him a history lesson. This lesson went back to the days of his grandfather Nebuchadnezzar and brought to the surface the problem that king had had with pride—a problem shared by his grandson Belshazzar (5:18–21).

Also, before Daniel interpreted the handwriting, he declared God's judgment on Belshazzar and confirmed that his sin was not a sin of ignorance: "You . . . have not humbled your heart, although you knew all this" (5:22).

The king's sin was not ignorance. It was . . .

78

- arrogance, seen in the king's defiant spirit;
- blasphemy, displayed in the king's defiling of the temple vessels;
- idolatry, evidenced by the king's idol-worship;
- rebellion, because the king refused to let God be God (5:23).

All of this deserved the judgment of God, and the handwritten message on the wall indicated that judgment was coming:

"MENE, MENE, TEKEL, UPHARSIN."

MENE: *God has numbered your kingdom, and finished it;*

TEKEL: You have been weighed in the balances, and found wanting;

PERES: Your kingdom has been divided, and given to the Medes and Persians (5:26–28).

Judgment was coming. There was no offer of relief or remedy; there was no way out, no loophole, no technicality—just the consequences of Belshazzar's foolish choices.

That very night Belshazzar, king of the Chaldeans, was slain. And Darius the Mede received the kingdom, being about sixty-two years old (5:30–31).

"That very night" the seemingly impenetrable walls of Babylon were penetrated by the Medo-Persian armies and the city fell. The historian Xenophon tells us that Cyrus' general, Gobryas, conquered Babylon by damming the river that flowed under the walls and through the heart of the city. Then the army marched under the walls and conquered the city.

Notice, however, that before Belshazzar was killed and his kingdom conquered, he ordered the rewards to be given to Daniel, including that he be made the third highest ruler in the kingdom.

"It is hard to have patience with people who say 'There is no death' or 'Death doesn't matter.' There is death. And whatever is matters. And whatever happens has consequences, and it and they are irrevocable and irreversible."
—C. S. LEWIS

80

*   *   *

Belshazzar, who was consumed by the same kind of pride that nearly destroyed his grandfather, tried to defy God. But he failed. The result was that he was "weighed in the balances, and found wanting." This raises a key question that each of us needs to answer: How do I measure up?

How do I measure up? Not in the eyes of the crowd but in the eyes of God?

What we must never forget is that we are first and foremost called to live before the Audience of One—not other people. May we so live that we measure up to God's design for our lives. To live, as Daniel did, to be measured only by the Lord.

It was that desire to please God, and God alone, that gave Daniel the courage to confront the king and rebuke him. It was the abiding presence of God in Daniel's life that brought him a steely resolve. And as Belshazzar's moral vacuum brought certain consequences into his life, Daniel's courage brought long-term results that included a legacy of character and faithfulness.

The immediate results? Well, Belshazzar did keep his word. Before he was killed and his kingdom conquered, he ordered the rewards to be given to Daniel.

> And they clothed Daniel with purple and put a chain of gold around his neck, and made a proclamation concerning him that he should be the third ruler in the kingdom (5:29).

Living a Life of Devotion

Daniel has spent almost his entire life in captivity in Babylon. He has served King Nebuchadnezzar, King Belshazzar, and is now serving Darius the Mede, who has set up his government in Babylon after the death of Belshazzar. Daniel has been appointed as one of the king's three governors over the entire realm (Daniel 6:1-2), and he soon distinguishes himself:

> Daniel distinguished himself above the governors and satraps, because an excellent spirit was in him; and the king gave thought to setting him over the whole realm (6:3).

Notice that this verse states that Daniel had an "excellent spirit" in him. It is the same phrase Queen Amytis used to describe Daniel (Daniel 5:12). Some view this as the presence of spiritual excellence in Daniel's life as an expression of his godly character. Others see it as a reference to his skills and abilities in being able to wisely manage the affairs of the kingdom. Still others see it as the consummation of all we have witnessed in his life—distinctiveness, confidence, concern, and courage.

Whatever the full nature of this "spirit," it was pivotal in advancing Daniel once again to a key position of honor and authority. However, such power and position invariably attract resentment and jealousy, and Daniel soon found himself a target of these emotions.

The Problem of Jealousy

So the governors and satraps sought to find some charge against Daniel concerning the

kingdom; but they could find no charge or
fault, because he was faithful; nor was there
any error or fault found in him. Then these
men said, "We shall not find any charge
against this Daniel unless we find it against
him concerning the law of his God."

So these governors and satraps thronged
before the king, and said thus to him:
"King Darius, live forever! All the governors
of the kingdom, the administrators and
satraps, the counselors and advisors, have
consulted together to establish a royal
statute and to make a firm decree, that
whoever petitions any god or man for thirty
days, except you, O king, shall be cast into
the den of lions. Now, O king, establish
the decree and sign the writing, so that it
cannot be changed, according to the law
of the Medes and Persians, which does not
alter."

Therefore King Darius signed the written decree (6:4–9).

The wonderful Scottish expositor of the 1800s, Alexander Maclaren, described the court of Darius as:

Half shambles and half pigsty. Luxury, sensuality, lust, self-seeking, idolatry, ruthlessness, cruelty and the like were the environment of this man. And in the middle of these there grew up that fair flower of character, pure and stainless, by the acknowledgement of enemies, and in which not accusers could find a speck or a spot. There are no circumstances in which a man must have his garments spotted by the world. However deep the filth through which he must wade, if God sent him there, and if he keeps hold of God's hand, his purity will be more stainless by reason of the impurity round him.

———

> *"Pride is essentially competitive. . . . Pride gets no pleasure out of having something, only out of having more of it than the next man. We say people are proud of being rich, or clever, or good-looking, but they are not. They are proud of being richer, or cleverer, or better-looking than others."*
> —C. S. LEWIS

These lower-level officials were much more attuned to the court of Darius than to the character of Daniel, and they despised Daniel because he now had authority over them. Pride is competitive, and envy is the result of wounded pride. These proud men were wounded by the elevation of this man of integrity, and they wanted to destroy him.

They looked for grounds on which to

87

accuse him, but they could not find any fault in him. Why? Because "he was faithful; nor was there any error or fault found in him" (6:4). In spite of living for years in an environment that was essentially a moral cesspool, Daniel had stayed pure.

Attacking someone of impeccable character is difficult, and these officials knew it.

> These men said, "We shall not find any charge against this Daniel unless we find it against him concerning the law of his God" (6:5).

Daniel's only perceivable point of weakness was his devotion to God. What a testimony— particularly coming from his enemies! The only way these conspirators could attack him was to attack his relationship with God.

The officials used deception to get what they

wanted, playing on Darius' pride. They asked
him to establish a law that would make it illegal
for the next thirty days to make a petition to any
god or man—except to Darius himself (6:6–8).
Since Darius himself was playing second fiddle to
Cyrus the Persian, this decree elevated him to the
position of a god and enhanced his own sense of
power, which Cyrus had limited.

And what would be the penalty for violating
this decree?

> "Whoever petitions any god or man for
> thirty days, except you, O king, shall be cast
> into the den of lions" (6:7).

The jealousy of these officials knew no
bounds. They wanted Daniel dead.

Darius signed the decree, and since this was
"the law of the Medes and Persians," it couldn't
be revoked. This explains why they wanted the

decree limited to thirty days. After Daniel was dead, they could get back to their normal lives.

Apparently, Darius was a good man. But, like all of us, he had weaknesses. In the heat of the moment, with his ego stroked, he made a rash decision and approved their law banning prayer.

"You cannot run away from a weakness; you must sometimes fight it out or perish. And if that be so, why not now, and where you stand?"
—ROBERT LOUIS STEVENSON

The Power of Testimony

Daniel was so devoted to God that obedience to Him was more important than obedience to unjust laws. This illustrates the biblical principle of obedient disobedience in which, when we must choose between obeying God's law or man's law, we choose to obey God's. In the New Testament

we see this principle practiced by the apostles
when they were commanded to stop preaching.
They said, "We ought to obey God rather than
men" (Acts 5:29).

> Now when Daniel knew that the writing
> was signed, he went home. And in his
> upper room, with his windows open toward
> Jerusalem, he knelt down on his knees three
> times that day, and prayed and gave thanks
> before his God, as was his custom since early
> days (6:10).

Daniel disobeyed the unjust law by praying
three times a day, just as he had done for years.
Daniel knew the secret of living a pure life in
the midst of an impure environment, and he was
unwilling to change or even appear to change to
satisfy the crowd.

Then these men assembled and found Daniel
praying and making supplication before his
God (6:11).

Daniel broke their law because it violated
God's law—and he was caught. But the fear of
being caught did not deter him. Daniel was
willing to accept the consequences of being
obedient to God.

92

This is a vital lesson for us, and it highlights
two things we need to keep in mind: (1) We must
be willing to accept the consequences for doing
the right thing. The apostle Peter said, "But even
if you should suffer for righteousness' sake, you
are blessed" (1 Peter 3:14). And (2) God is still in
control, even when life unfairly banishes us to the
proverbial lions' den.

Daniel was caught praying to God, and he
would suffer for righteousness' sake. But he was
prepared to glorify God.

The Peace of God

And they went before the king, and spoke concerning the king's decree: "Have you not signed a decree that every man who petitions any god or man within thirty days, except you, O king, shall be cast into the den of lions?"

The king answered and said, "The thing is true, according to the law of the Medes and Persians, which does not alter."

So they answered and said before the king, "That Daniel, who is one of the captives from Judah, does not show due regard for you, O king, or for the decree that you have signed, but makes his petition three times a day" (6:12–13).

These men were certainly sly. First, they reminded Darius of his irrevocable decree. Then they leveled their attack with an accusation that was a mix of truth and slander. Daniel had not disregarded the king, but he did refuse to disregard his God.

> And the king, when he heard these words, was greatly displeased with himself, and set his heart on Daniel to deliver him; and he labored till the going down of the sun to deliver him.
> Then these men approached the king, and said to the king, "Know, O king, that it is the law of the Medes and Persians that no decree or statute which the king establishes may be changed" (6:14-15).

Darius' response shows that he finally understood what was going on, for he was "greatly displeased with himself." He realized that he had exercised poor judgment. It seems that he was not displeased with Daniel or with Daniel's behavior, but with his own pride.

Darius pursued Daniel's release because he didn't want him to suffer the consequences of the foolish decree. He looked for a legal loophole, but there was none. Darius was trapped by his own law. There was no way out—Daniel had to be executed.

> So the king gave the command, and they brought Daniel and cast him into the den of lions. But the king spoke, saying to Daniel, "Your God, whom you serve continually, He will deliver you." Then a stone was brought and laid on the mouth of the den, and the king sealed it with his own signet ring and with the signets of his lords, that the purpose concerning Daniel might not be changed (6:16-17).

Having been found guilty of the crime of serving God continually, Daniel was cast into the lions' den. This particular form of punishment was a horrible death. The lions were usually starved, mistreated, and taunted so they would rip a man to pieces.

In desperation, Darius tried to offer a final consolation to Daniel: "Your God will deliver you." Unfortunately, it does not seem likely that this statement was born of faith, but out of fatalism.

Have you ever wondered what happened inside the lions' den once the stone was sealed? Donald K. Campbell, in *Daniel: Decoder of Dreams*, quotes *The Prophet-Statesman*, which suggests that the scene may have unfolded this way:

> As the guards closed the aperture and went their way, Daniel slid gradually to the floor of the den. The big lions that had come bounding from their caverns at the inflow of light, all stopped suddenly short as a steed

reined up by a powerful hand on a bridle. The initial roars died away as they formed a solid phalanx and looked toward this man who stood in their den in easy reach. There was some snorting, and a little whining, and some of them turned around and went back to their caverns. Others of the great beasts yawned and lay down on the floor, but not one made a move to advance toward their visitor. "Thanks be unto Jehovah," breathed the prophet. "He hath stopped the mouths of these fierce beasts that they will do me no harm."

He sat down on the floor of the den and leaned his back against the wall to make himself comfortable for the night. Soon two cub lions moved in his direction, not stealthily or crouching as though to make an attack, but in obvious friendliness, and one lay on each side of Daniel as though

to give him warmth and protection in the
chilly dungeon. Presently their mother, an
old lioness, crept over and lay in front of the
prophet. He gently stroked their backs as they
each turned their heads and licked his hands.
Enclosed by the lioness and her cubs, the
head of the patriarch was gradually pillowed
on the back of one of the cubs, as the four
slept soundly in perfect peace and tranquility.

The Protection of God

Daniel may have been sleeping peacefully with
the lions, but the conscience-stricken Darius
passed a very different kind of night.

Now the king went to his palace and spent
the night fasting; and no musicians were
brought before him. Also his sleep went from
him (6:18).

Worry, guilt, loss of appetite, loss of sleep—all
were the effects of Darius' failure to discern the evil
conspiracy of his officials. Finally, after a sleepless
night, the king rose and went to the den of lions.

> When he came to the den, he cried out with
> a lamenting voice to Daniel. The king spoke,
> saying to Daniel, "Daniel, servant of the
> living God, has your God, whom you serve
> continually, been able to deliver you from the
> lions?"
>
> Then Daniel said to the king, "O king,
> live forever! My God sent His angel and shut
> the lions' mouths, so that they have not hurt
> me, because I was found innocent before
> Him; and also, O king, I have done no wrong
> before you."
>
> Now the king was exceedingly glad for
> him, and commanded that they should
> take Daniel up out of the den. So Daniel

was taken up out of the den, and no injury
whatever was found on him, because he
believed in his God (6:20-23).

Even in the words of Darius, we see the
profound impact that Daniel's life has had on
this man: "Has your God, whom you serve
continually, been able to deliver you from the
lions?" It's amazing that Darius even considered
the possibility that God had protected Daniel
from the lions. Then, from out of the darkness,
came Daniel's calm, confident reply that God,
indeed, had protected him.

Daniel was not hurt "because he believed in
his God" (6:23). Hebrews 11:33 also tells us that
it was Daniel's faith that "stopped the mouths
of lions." Of course, as Hebrews 11:35-40
indicates, it's not always God's will to deliver
His children. In the early church, thousands
of martyrs were fed to lions and ushered into

eternity. But whether or not God delivers at any particular moment, His ability to deliver is never diminished. He is always able.

The Power of Priority

And the king gave the command, and they brought those men who had accused Daniel, and they cast them into the den of lions— them, their children, and their wives; and the lions overpowered them, and broke all their bones in pieces before they ever came to the bottom of the den (6:24).

Just as Haman, in the book of Esther, was hanged on his own gallows, so Daniel's accusers were cast into the lions' den where they suffered the fate they had intended for Daniel. And in an even much stronger statement of faith than the one Nebuchadnezzar gave (4:34–35, 37), King Darius wrote:

To all peoples, nations, and languages that
dwell in all the earth: Peace be multiplied to
you. I make a decree that in every dominion
of my kingdom men must tremble and fear
before the God of Daniel. For He is the living
God, and steadfast forever; His kingdom is
the one which shall not be destroyed, and His
dominion shall endure to the end. He delivers
and rescues, and He works signs and wonders
in heaven and on earth, who has delivered
Daniel from the power of the lions (6:25–27).

As for Daniel, his story ends happily:

So this Daniel prospered in the reign of
Darius and in the reign of Cyrus the Persian
(6:28).

Daniel was the embodiment of Psalm 1:3: "He
shall be like a tree planted by the rivers of water,

that brings forth its fruit in its season, whose leaf also shall not wither; and whatever he does shall prosper." God had truly blessed Daniel.

When he was in the midst of living his life, however, Daniel had no idea what the outcome would be. He knew God's promises and power, but he didn't know God's plan. He only knew that he wanted to live a life of obedience that honored his God, no matter what the situation or circumstances, no matter what the trial or temptation.

Daniel also knew that he couldn't survive without prayer. It's been said that God's Word is the milk, meat, and bread of life, but prayer is its breath. You can live for a long period of time without food, but you can't survive more than a few minutes without breath. That's how important prayer is.

Do you give prayer that kind of priority in your life?

*   *   *

We are living in a Babylonian-like world. We are surrounded by an ever-changing, morally ambiguous, deeply troubled, and constantly deteriorating culture. Yet it is in this kind of a world that we are called to be the Daniels of our own generation. We can either be poured into the mold of our culture, or, like Daniel, we can use the darkness as an opportunity to reflect the light of our God.

As we live our daily lives, Daniel's obedient life of distinction, confidence, concern, courage, and devotion are a wonderful example and legacy for us to follow.

The choice is yours. How will you serve God in your generation?

FOR PERSONAL REFLECTION

NOTES

NOTES

FOR PERSONAL REFLECTION

NOTES

FOR PERSONAL REFLECTION

NOTES